This book is dedicated to you.

THOUGHTS
for the
LONELY NIGHTS
a conversation about grief

InSight Books, Inc
Oklahoma City

Thoughts for the Lonely Nights
A Conversation About Grief
Doug Manning
Third Edtion © 2013

First Edition © 2000

InSight Books, Inc
PO Box 42467
Oklahoma City, Oklahoma 73123
800.658.9262 or 405.810.9501
www.insightbooks.com
orders&info@insightbooks.com

Cover Photo: Digital West, Oklahoma City, Oklahoma

Manufactured in the United States of America

ISBN 978-1-892785-36-7

BOOKS · RESOURCES · TRAINING

Touching Lives. Creating Memories.

Contents

Introduction

When I first began writing about grief there were very few books on the subject. Now there are thousands of helpful books available. These books seem to fit into three categories. Some are personal experiences describing a very personal grief journey after the loss of a loved one. Some are explanations of the grieving process. Still others are clinical studies about grieving written for professionals who give counsel to those in grief.

I hope this book will be different. There will be some shared experiences used to illustrate. There will be some brief descriptions about the grieving process, but not in any detail. Most people in grief will have access to books that do a great job in these areas. This book will concentrate on the impact of grief. The feelings, questions and needs felt during the struggle to survive a loss.

I call this *Thoughts For The Lonely Nights* because I envisioned sitting with you in a room late at night and simply having a conversation. I wrote out what I would say on certain elements of grief and then left room for you to write out what you would say back. This makes the book somewhat like a journal of your grief but not as formal as the usual journal. My hope is we will produce a written conversation about your grieving experience. The best part of this book will be either written or spoken by you, not me.

Thank you for the opportunity.

Doug Manning

Section I

Feelings

*For two years I was just as crazy as
you can be and still be at large.
I didn't have any really
normal minutes
during those two years.
It wasn't just grief. It was total
confusion. I was nutty, and that's the
truth. How did I come out of it? I don't
know, because I didn't know when I was
in it that I was in it.*
—Helen Hayes on the death of
her husband, Charles MacArthur

Lonely to the Bone

Grief, by its very nature, is lonely. Lonely, by its very nature, produces grieving. People in grief feel a loneliness that goes to the bone.

Friends are wonderful and you could not make it without them but they cannot make the lonely go away.

A mate can hold you in the night and cry as you cry, but the lonely does not go away.

Family can be devastated along with you, but it is still lonely.

The loneliness may be difficult for you to understand. "Why am I so lonely? I share how I feel, I don't hide my pain, I talk about my loss, and still the loneliness goes to my very soul."

And you may get angry about the loneliness. "My mate, of all people, should understand how I feel, and should touch all the right spots and fill the dark places. If he/she can't, do we really have anything going on in our lives together?"

And, the struggle can dominate your time and energy. You may spend your time either thinking about how lonely you are, or trying to find a way to make it go away.

And, worst of all you may end up deciding you are weak and are just holding gigantic pity parties for yourself, that you should stop feeling sorry for yourself and get on with living. The telling and the fussing do no good, it is still lonely.

Feelings Too Deep

You are lonely because you are faced with the impossible task of explaining feelings and the only tools you have to do that with are words. There is no way that can be done. How can anyone explain a feeling? Can love be described in words? Can fear? Can anyone describe how it felt the first time they held their newborn? Neither can you describe how you feel now.

> You want to.
> You need to.
> And you will try with all of your might.
> But words are not adequate for the task.

Caught Between Words

Even when we try to explain our feelings, we often get blocked by the lack of words to use. A mother told me her son had died as a result of a gun going off during a party. She said she had a terrible struggle with the word "accident." To her an accident was the result of some act of nature or a car wreck. Every time she would say she did not call it an accident, everyone would immediately ask if she thought it was murder. This became increasingly troubling to her and blocked her progress in grieving. She visited with one of her son's friends who had been present at the party. When she told him she had a hard time with the word accident he sighed and said, "Me too." She began to heal that day. Someone else had the same struggle and could not explain how he felt.

Still Good News

Hearing that the loneliness will not go away does not sound like good news or words of comfort, but this news can be a great deal of help and comfort. Accepting that there is really no way to get rid of the loneliness can help you focus your energy on dealing with it instead of desperately seeking a cure. This news can help couples accept that their mates cannot fully understand how they feel. Then they can concentrate on finding other ways to give and receive support.

You can then spend your effort on understanding yourself, exploring your feelings, and learning that you are normal. Then you can concentrate on finding outlets for your feelings that you are comfortable with, and that fit your needs.

This book serves two purposes. Hopefully it will give thoughts that help you make it through the lonely times. It also leaves room for writing out your own thoughts. Keeping a journal is one of the healthy and healing ways of dealing with the loneliness. Writing down how you feel clarifies those feelings and, in the simple expression, you may find peace. The important words in this book are yet to be written.

Thoughts For the Lonely Nights

Grief is a very anti-social state.
—Penelope Mortimer

Neither Friend Nor Foe

It is hard to believe how much physical pain is caused by grieving. You expect the emotional and mental suffering, but somehow you don't expect your chest to feel like you have been in a car wreck and every bone in your body to ache.

No one would welcome the pain. No one would call it a friend and yet it is in the pain—in the times when we hurt the most—that we are healing. Grief is not an enemy to be avoided. It is a process to be walked through. The best thing to do with grief is grieve.

You are doing your best grief work when you hurt the most. That sounds backwards. That even sounds cruel and unfeeling, but the pain is there because you are dealing with your feelings. Dealing with feelings hurts, but that is the pathway toward coping with your loss.

Grief works much like a bad cold. A cold creates mucus that fills our sinuses to the breaking point. The mucus must find a way to be released. Some people try to dry the mucus up with medication and it seems to work for a time, but when the medication wears off the mucus flows again. Sometimes the mucus internalizes and flows down our throat causing other problems like bronchitis and respiratory problems. Some times we can relieve the pressure by simply blowing our nose. That is not a pleasant experience, and if we do it often enough the nose becomes very sore, but it does relieve the pressure.

Now it may be silly for me to compare grief with the common cold, but the analogy has some merit. Grief creates its own mucus inside your soul. You can try to beat it down with medication or alcohol but when these wear off the pain is still there waiting for you. You can internalize it and let it take its toll on your whole being. Or you can learn to let it out.

Letting it out is not pleasant. Letting it out will be much harder for some than it is for others. Letting it out will often be a lonely proposition since it is often hard to find anyone you can feel comfortable enough with to allow them to witness such a thing.

You may fear you will seem weak and too emotional. You may feel no one wants to endure your tears and tirades. But when the pain gets intense enough you will not care who is watching or what they think, you will let it out. In that case and that case alone, the pain is not your enemy.

Grief comes in waves. The waves come without warning and without pattern. Suddenly we are overwhelmed with grief and pain. We cry at the oddest times. We break down in the most embarrassing of places. There are some times when we can expect a wave to hit; times like anniversaries of birth, death or marriage, times like the holidays or special times of the year; some will be swallowed up by the summer or maybe the fall of the year, or every year when they have the fair, but, most of the time, waves just happen. They hit, we hurt, and they subside a little. Gradually, over time the waves are not as high, they don't last as long, and they come less often. The waves come to remind you that it is time to focus again on the healing of your soul.

Healing is a process of embracing the pain and crying the wave dry.

Thoughts For the Lonely Nights

Dear Lord, be good to me
Your sea is so wide and my boat is so small.
The Mariners' Prayer

Thoughts For the Lonely Nights

Will I Survive This Pain?

There will be times when no one can convince you that you will survive. The pain is far too intense for you to see any hope. The loss is so overwhelming that you think you will die from the sheer loneliness alone. During the early part of grief the overriding question is, "Will I survive this pain?" "Will I be able to stand it?" There is no easy answer to that question.

A young mother told me that her pastor's response when she asked that question was, "Well, sure you will. Everyone else does." She is still angry at his flippant response.

Your heart has been broken. It is not going to mend. A chunk has been bitten out of it and it will not grow back. You will never be back to normal. You will always miss the person and you will always hurt. The best I can promise is that the pain you feel right now will one day be a dull ache, but it will ache as long as you live.

Hopefully you will survive. Hopefully you will find the support you need to survive with your being still intact. That does not mean it will not be a daily struggle for a time. That does not mean you will not be scarred in the process. That does not mean you will someday be able to just forget and move on.

Grief is a natural response to loss. It is nature's way of healing a broken heart. But it is a process. You are on a journey through a mine field of emotions and pain working your way slowly toward the other side. There are some things you can do to help insure your survival. Such things as:

Giving Yourself Permission To Grieve

One of the hardest parts of grieving is allowing yourself the right to grieve. If you broke a leg, you would have the leg set and placed in a cast. There would be no resistance on your part to having the leg placed in a cast. If the doctor said you had to wear the cast for eight weeks, you would not feel weak or silly because the leg did not heal in two weeks. If, at the end of eight weeks, the doctor said the leg needed more time to heal you would not wonder if you were some kind of freak. You would just wear the cast until the leg healed.

But a broken heart is a different thing. We somehow think we should be able to get over this hurt with kind words and a few tears. So we resist the grieving. We pressure ourselves to be better than we are. We are embarrassed to "still be crying after all of this time." The more we pressure the harder it is to move through the process.

Giving yourself permission to hurt is one step toward survival. The other is to give yourself permission to say you hurt. Far too often we think others will think we are weak or have very little faith if we grieve too much. Far too often our friends will let us know that we are wallowing in our grief and should get ahold of ourselves. Far too often we stop letting people know we hurt to impress them with our dignity and strength.

I wish Jackie Kennedy had cried at President Kennedy's funeral. We have the vision of her standing on the steps of the Capitol and John John saluting his father. The whole world seemed to stand in awe and exclaim, "What dignity, what strength, what class under pressure." It may have been all of those things, but it was also a terrible way to survive the pain of grief.

You work through your grief when you allow yourself the permission to do so. You work through your grief when you talk about it. Matter of fact, I think you must talk grief to death. You talk until you are through talking. You should not let anyone, including yourself, take that away from you.

A cut finger—
> *is numb before it bleeds,*
> *it bleeds before it hurts,*
> *it hurts until it begins to heal,*
> *it forms a scab and itches until finally,*
>> *the scab is gone and a small scar*
>> *is left where once there was a wound.*

Grief is the deepest wound you have ever had.
> *Like a cut finger, it goes through stages*
> *and leaves a scar.*

Normal

I love the word *NORMAL*. If I have a calling in life it is to run around convincing people that they are normal. Most of us don't think we are. Most of us believe that we think and feel things no one else thinks or feels. Most of us think if someone could really see inside of us and know what we were thinking or feeling they would probably have us committed or, at least, ostracized from society.

We do not think we are normal because no one knows what normal is. How are we supposed to feel or react to the things we experience in life? When is it proper to be angry, or fearful, or happy? Since we really don't know we tend to assume we don't do it like everyone else. The longer I live the more I am convinced we are all about alike. We are probably normal.

If we don't feel normal at normal times, we certainly don't feel normal when we are in grief. Every emotion is in turmoil. Your mind is overloaded until you suffer from brownout. You get lost in the grocery store. You forget where you are driving. You can't remember appointments. After my brother died, my sister-in-law called to tell me she had found her lamp. She had two lamps in her bedroom and one had been missing. She said she had looked all over the house for weeks trying to find the lamp. She had found it that night, in the den. She had been reading by it night after night. She said she had turned it off and gone looking for it many a time. She called to see if I thought she had lost her mind. Brownout means you forget and forget that you forgot.

You may cry at things you think you should laugh at. You can get angry over nothing at all. Your feelings are already hurt, so anything can bring them to the surface in pain. This may leave you wondering if you are losing your mind. Has the loss been too much? Did I not survive?

You need to avoid the "Feel bad because you feel bad syndrome." That happens when you have a feeling you don't think you should have. Then you think there is something wrong with you or those feelings would not be there. Then you conclude that there is something wrong with you and the intensity grows like a rolling snowball.

In grief there is no such thing as normal. We all go through grief in our own unique way and on our own schedule. Grief is as unique as a fingerprint. There are no experts in grief. The person who has been through grief is an expert in his or her grief, but they don't know how anyone else should feel or react. The only "normal" you should worry about is what is normal for you. And then relax.

The best advice I can give is *feel what you feel.* You cannot change these feelings, so just feel them. I get call after call from people who ask if it is all right to feel the way they do. In every case I say the same thing, "Feel what you feel, and do so in peace." What you feel ain't normal for anyone else, but it is normal for you.

I measure every Grief I meet
With narrow, probing Eyes—
I wonder if it weights like Mine
Or has an Easier size
              –Emily Dickinson

Thoughts For the Lonely Nights

Where Am I?

I started writing about grief in 1977. I read everything I could find on the subject before I put pen to paper. At the time, that was three books. Now there are thousands of books. Where once we did not study the subject at all, now we may be in danger of over studying and over structuring the process. If we are not careful we will stereotype grief into some set pattern that everyone must follow or else they are not healthy. In the process we can make grieving more difficult to understand and to work through.

There Are No Stages

Almost every book about grief talks about the "stages" we experience. In my book *Don't Take My Grief Away From Me* I presented grief in four stages when I first published it. They were Shock, Reality, Reaction, and Reconstruction. Even at that early date I did not like the idea of stages. They seemed far too clear-cut to me. They were like lines of demarcation: "I was in Stage Two until yesterday at six and then I passed into Stage Three." This led to far too much time being spent trying to define which stage a person was in.

I really don't think it works that way. I think we flip-flop through the process. I think we can be in Stage Three this morning and back in Stage Two by afternoon. Matter of fact, we can be in two stages at the same time. The stages are just general descriptions of some of the feelings most people experience as they progress through the process of grief. They are not some kind of rigid steps we must take in some kind of order. Who knows when a feeling will surface? Everyone will experience these feelings in their own way and on their own schedule.

I often use the analogy that grief is like peeling an onion–it comes off one layer at a time and you cry a lot. I like that analogy because it gives such flexibility to the process. If I gave an audience of five hundred people each an onion, every person would deal with the onion in a different manner. Some would peel it with great speed and gusto, some would be so dainty and slow the onion would be in danger of disintegrating before the job was finished. We grieve in the same way we peel onions. We have our own method for solving problems and facing hurts. Grief is not the time for having new methods forced upon us.

In general terms there is a period of time when you are in a state of shock. It is real but also unreal. It is like a nightmare that seems horrible, but you will wake up in a little while, and it will all be gone.

This time can best be described as a whirl. The outer layer of the onion is a dry hull that can be crushed into confetti. If this confetti is thrown in the air it can be a good picture of the whirl–thousands of questions are whirling in your mind. They hit and run. You think of them, and they are gone. Reality is whirling in the mix but it does not land long enough for you to deal with it. When my brother died, I would think that I would never see him again but, before I could even cry, that thought was gone and another took its place.

There may seem to be two tracks running through your head. One track is telling you that you have been devastated and will not be able to survive the pain. The other track is angry enough to want to jerk God out of Heaven and demand an explanation. You may be constantly jumping tracks. You feel helpless one moment and frustrated the next.

The question is "How long should the whirl last?" "What is normal?" I hate to quote Yogi Bera who said, "It ain't over till it's over," but that is really true. The whirl will last until it is over. There are no time frames. There are no limits. And the length of time it takes does not reflect on the person. Longer does not mean you loved the person more. Longer does not mean you are weak. Longer does not mean you do not have adequate faith. Longer means this is how you peel onions.

The whirl is the mind's way of protecting itself from a breakdown. No one is capable of processing the shock of a grieving experience until they have had a time to prepare. The whirl is the preparation time. You are numb because you need to be numb. The whirl is the calm before the storm, and you need it desperately.

During the whirl your concentration may not be strong enough to do much writing. This may be the time for writing down random thoughts and questions that will be revisited at a later time.

Thoughts For the Lonely Nights

*It isn't for the moment you are struck that
you need courage,
but for the long, uphill climb back to sanity
and faith and security.*
—Anne Morrow Lindbergh
Hour of Gold, Hour of Lead

The Loneliest of Times

The whirl is a time of great protection before the loneliest time of all begins to dawn. Some call this the time of reality. Others have titles for what is their defined stage of grief. Basically, the numb wears off and the hurting begins.

You wake up in the night with the awful realization that you will never see this person again. A deep sense of foreboding moves into your very being and it will not go away. Your chest hurts and you can't breathe. You call a friend but don't know what to say when they answer. You cry until you are sure there are no more tears left, and then you cry some more.

They call the first stage "shock," but this is when you are really shocked. It has been a period of some weeks since the death happened and you have been amazed at how well you have been doing. You have hurt of course, but overall you have been able to function. You may have even gone back to work and tried to settle into the old routines. You have known the truth, but you still expected the door to open and your loved one to walk back into your life. It has been real but not real—like watching a sad movie. You cry, but you know the credits will roll, the lights will come on, and you will discover it was all make-believe. This time the lights don't come on, and no credits roll on the screen. You realize this time it is for real. And you crash.

I wish there was some magic formula to make you feel better right now. I wish there were wonderful words that would change your feelings. I wish there was some beautiful way of thinking that would make your pain go away. This must be walked through. You can't go around it. You can't anesthetize yourself so it won't hurt. There are no short cuts. This is the hard layer of grief's onion.

It is faint comfort to know that you are making the most progress through your grief when you are hurting the worst. You want the hurt to stop. Knowing you are normal helps a little, but it doesn't relieve the pain.

During this hard time, you need what I call "the three H's." You need people who will *Hang Around, Hug You, and Hush.* Even though they cannot know what you feel, it helps to have people who will just be there. You need to find friends who will come when you call. Let them know that all you need is their presence. They don't have to know what to say. They don't have to be trained. All they have to be is there.

Hugs are wonderful. The two most important elements to walking through the grief journey are hugs and tears. Warm, loving arms give strength when there is nothing left inside of you to fight with. The love of a friend or a mate can be the only thing you can hang on to during this time of terror.

Silence is golden. People who have been through grief often complain about people who talked too much; they report wanting to grab their ears to shut out the noise. You will naturally be drawn to those friends or family members who will just be there. You may be reluctant to be around many other friends or family. This is not the time to worry about a few hurt feelings. When you are here at the bottom, use the ones who help and avoid the ones who hurt.

When I close my eyes as I write this, I envision you sitting in a darkened room late at night. You can't sleep and you don't want to waken the rest of the family. Television seems so silly at a time like this. You find it hard to read more than a few lines and then you forget them almost as soon as they are read. Maybe it will help to stop and listen to some quiet music while you sort through what you are feeling right now. May I urge you to write out your thoughts? They may not be coherent. There may be more questions than thoughts. The pain and loss may be all you can write about. But, there is something powerful about putting it on paper.

Thoughts For the Lonely Nights

Death ends a life but it does not end the relationship which struggles in the survivor's mind towards some final resolution, some clear meaning, which it perhaps never finds.
—Robert W. Anderson,
I Never Sang for My Father

And Then Came the Anger

Are you mad yet? There is anger in grief, and there should be. Anger is the natural response to hurt and you have been hurt. You may not recognize the anger. Many people tell me they do not remember feeling angry during their grief. They do remember feeling frustrated, upset, and hurt but not angry.

Most of us were raised thinking that anger was bad, that anger was the pseudonym for hate. We were trained to hold in our anger and deny its existence. When deep hurts come we tend to continue this process. We substitute other words for anger, but these feelings all come from the same emotional roots as anger, so let's just say you probably are angry, and you should be.

The anger is healthy. It is the driving force that propels us through our grief. We hit bottom, get mad, and begin to fight our way back. If we return to the analogy of grief being like peeling an onion, the thing that pushes us from the hard reality layer of the onion to the fighting back layer I call the "reaction layer" is anger.

Most of the intense feelings stirring inside of you are the results of anger. You may feel as if you are going to explode. You may find yourself out of control over simple things that once you would not have noticed. Even close friends may easily hurt your feelings. You may feel a great deal of guilt that will not go away. These are the signs of anger that needs to escape.

Even though the anger you feel is healthy, you still need to deal with it. Swallowed anger does not go away, it seethes inside until it finds an outlet in illness or depression. There are several suggestions you might try to bleed off some of the anger.

Keep Your Cussin' Current

To me there is *cursing,* which is using foul and abusive language, and there is *cussin',* which I define as expressing deep feelings with whatever language you are comfortable with. You need to keep your cussin' current. If something makes you angry, say so. If you get up in the morning and do not like anything or anybody, tell the world. If friends are letting you down, gripe your head off. If your mate is failing to be sensitive, express what you need in no uncertain terms. This is not the time to be the sweet person who is always "fine." This is the time to say what is bugging you.

Find a Friend—A Safe Friend

The only way to keep your cussin' current is to find a safe person to unload on; a friend who will not think less of you, a person who will not hear and tell, a person that will share their pain with you if there is such a need. That person may be a current friend, or you may need to meet new friends who are more comfortable with your pain. Grief support groups are a wonderful resource for finding safe friends. They have been there and will understand. Your mate probably will not be able to fill this role. You certainly should talk to your mate as much as he or she is willing to talk. However, sometimes the unloading must be about the mate. If you have lost your mate, then that void seems even harder to fill. In grief you need safe people in a safe place. You need a person and a place where you can say anything and be accepted and loved.

Get Physical

Sometimes you will find it helpful to express your grief physically. Hit something, scream, bite...whatever feels good. There is a wonderful facility called *The Kids' Place,* it is a center for grieving children built after the bombing in Oklahoma City. The center has a room in the basement called "The Emotion Commotion Room." This room is sound proof and fully padded. It is equipped with Nerf bats and a punching bag. When the kids need to express their feelings, they go to the room and let it all out. They bang and scream and punch until they have found some relief.

I know a woman who buys cheap dishes from garage sales. When she needs a release she breaks them into the garbage container on her street. You may think that is too radical or you may wonder why you haven't already thought of that, but in some way you need just such an outlet for the feelings that must get out before they can go away.

List the Angers

Before we proceed to more exploration about anger in grief, it will be helpful if you could write down the things that make you angry. Maybe list them in categories such as the things that irritate, the things that upset, the things that make you angry, and the things that make you livid. Getting them in mind is the first step toward finding ways to get them out.

Thoughts For the Lonely Nights

*While grief is fresh, every attempt
to divert only irritates. You must
wait till it be digested...*
–Samuel Johnson

The Focus of Anger

Anger does not float well. It is not enough to be angry, we need to be angry at something or someone. The anger of grief will find a place. You will probably be angry at someone and at something during your grief journey. Being angry will not mean you are out of control. Being angry will not mean you have become some kind of undesirable person.

When the anger hits, you may become afraid that you will feel this way for the rest of your life. The anger is not permanent. Grief is transition, where you are today is not where you will be tomorrow. What you are mad about or at today is not necessarily what you will be mad about in a few weeks. There is no need to panic. But there is a need to understand what is happening to you, and to see where your anger is focusing. Anger can take many forms and focus on many things. May I suggest a few with the hope that you will either find the focus of your anger listed, or at least start the search toward your unique focus?

When the Anger is Irrational

Sometimes anger focuses irrationally. You may get angry at someone who had little or nothing to do with the loss. Quite often your anger will be out of proportion. You may get angry at a friend over some small incident you normally would not even notice. Anger can be like a heat seeking missile looking for the nearest target.

If you are a widow or widower you may well be angry at your mate for dying. They may or may not have had any part in the death. I have often heard reports like a widow who recently said, "I can't tell you how many times I have stood in the den and screamed out 'How could you leave me like this?' Then I just know I am going crazy."

If this is how you are reacting, relax. You are not going crazy. The anger must go somewhere and this is a very good place for it to go. You can fuss at your mate and love them at the same time. You want to think about them and talk to them anyway, so let them carry part of the load of the frustration and hurt you feel also.

When You are Mad at Those Who Serve

You may find yourself angry at those you expected to serve and somehow they did not function to your expectations; the physician who would not spend the time to even inform you, much less give any comfort. Or perhaps you think he/she failed in some more serious manner. There is no denying that mistakes are made and malpractice happens. I do think it wise to wait a while before you start filing lawsuits. The focus of anger may move to someone else and you will no longer feel as strongly as you do now. With that said, there is nothing wrong with being angry with the physician. The only problem is finding adequate ways of expressing the anger. It is hard to do this on a face-to-face basis with the physician so you end up having to unload on friends or lawyers. Even if you win the lawsuit, you still haven't gotten satisfaction.

Or, you may be angry with the clergy person and the members of your church. Too often they are with you until the funeral is over and then you feel abandoned and alone. I have no defense to offer. I could say they have not been there and therefore do not understand, but they should understand. Too many books have been written, too many programs given, for any of us not to know that people in grief need friends. This, too, is not a bad place for your anger to land.

When You are Mad at God

How do you feel about God? That He let you down? That He turned His back on you? That He could have kept this from happening and did not do so? God may well be the number one recipient of the anger we have in grief. This, too, is not a bad place for anger to focus. It may scare some of your friends or your minister, but it really is quite healthy. God is big enough to handle your anger.

A minister stood up in a recent conference and said, "I have told people for years that God will send His angels to watch over us. Then my daughter was killed in a car wreck and I am left wondering where He was that night." God has been so often presented as the protector from all the bad things that might happen to us. When bad things come we are confused and angry. "Why me?" is not the ranting of a weak faith, it is the legitimate question of a person who has suffered a deep loss.

These angers need expressing. As we said before we must keep our cussin' current. It is all right for your anger to focus on one of these or anywhere else it chooses. Holding in these feelings is not all right. Now is the time to feel what you feel and let it out.

The truth is that by and large, no matter how calm and controlled and accepting a face she may present to the world, a new widow is miserable and can be a very difficult creature.
—Joyce Brothers
Widowed

When You Are Mad at Your Mate

We seem to have a romanticized view of grief causing our marriages, and relationships to grow stronger and deeper. The idea is that we would cling together in our pain and find strength in numbers to face the storm. In the movies we would come out on the other side smiling and much more in love. The truth is that grief is hard on every relationship we have. That comes as a shock to us and we feel abandoned right when we have the most need. Instead of feeling great support and deepening love, you may be having a real struggle relating to your mate. You may even be wondering if the relationship can make it. This strain on your relationship does not mean you have a bad mate. The strain is the natural result of the grieving experience.

Grieving forces all of us to live in survival mode. Our first and foremost concern is our own survival. We are dominated by our own needs and our own pain. It is very difficult to find the energy to be concerned about anyone else's problems. This sounds selfish and inconsiderate, but it is neither. When we are under threat, the strongest instinct we have is self-preservation. We must first try to survive. We might tell ourselves that we should think of others, but we are the number one concern and we should be. Your first task is to survive. You may be self-interested and cranky and sound like a whining child, but you must survive. This instinct for survival creates a great deal of the strain. When it becomes clear that we will survive, then we can turn outward and begin to notice the needs of others.

Your mate is the most natural place for your anger to focus. A mate is supposed to be there for you. A mate is supposed to understand. A mate is supposed to take away the hurts. A mate is supposed to feel the same as you feel and react the same way you react. When any of these do not happen, there is anger. Often irrational, sometimes loud and explosive, other times quiet and seething, but in some form or other, the anger usually lands on the mate.

The expectations of relationships are usually so high that no one can fulfill them. Unfulfilled expectations are one of the root causes for divorce. In grief, these expectations become even higher and more important. When you hurt, you want help on your timetable and your mate is expected to know what to do and when to do it. Your temper is already on edge, so any slight misstep and you are ready to explode. The tension becomes almost unbearable.

Men and women grieve on different schedules. Women tend to be more comfortable dealing with feelings and can plunge into their grief immediately. Men seem to need to go off and "cave" for a little while before they are ready to share their feelings or listen to others. The wife can feel rejected and alone. The husband can feel like he is being pressured to conform to her way of grieving. Wedges can be driven into the relationship that can cause the loneliness to grow.

Intimacy suffers during grief. The differences between the sexes can, again, have an affect. Since sex in the male is more of a physical urge, the man's need for and interest in sex will probably not be affected. Sex to a woman is much more of an emotional expression and she has no emotions to give. She feels totally empty and cannot understand how her mate could even think of such things at a time like this. This can furnish a battleground for the couple to use for expressing all kinds of anger and frustrations.

So here you sit tonight...lonely and mad because you are lonely? Feeling like your mate, of all people, should understand how you feel without you having to say anything? Feeling rejected in your time of greatest need? I wish I could say, "go wake your mate up, kiss them, tell them how you feel, and everything will be all right." Kissing and telling how you feel is a good idea, but don't expect the anger to disappear with one kiss. It may take many sessions of kissing and telling. It may take some time.

It will help if you can take a look at your expectations. What are you wanting or needing that your mate is not providing? It might also help if you could write down exactly how your mate is failing to meet these expectations. Writing it down may clarify how much of the anger is deserved and how much is the result of anger's need to focus somewhere and your mate is there. Writing it down will also help you sort out those areas that are really impossible for anyone to meet.

There are always two sides, so maybe it will help if you write down what expectations your mate might have for you and how you might be failing to meet these needs. Remember your mate may also be feeling lonely and in need.

It will also be helpful to list the positive areas of help. The ways your mate is helping and responding to your needs. Sometimes all we can see is the negative and it overwhelms us.

Realizing that you need more help than your mate can give will also give some relief to the strain. No one can meet all of your needs when life is going along at normal pace. When you are in grief, that is made even more acutely so. You need a support system among people outside of your home. These people must take up the slack. During grief a couple must be willing to accept the limits to the help a mate can give. Accept what help is offered, and recognize that the relationship will build back after the storm.

Then, and this is the tough part, it might help for you and your mate to read or listen to this together and use it as an opening for a discussion of needs. A frank discussion about intimacy might need to be on the top of the list. Both of you need intimacy right now more than ever, but you may need to find new ways to express your intimacy for this period.

One last word; it is easier to act your way to a new way of feeling than it is to feel your way to a new way of acting. If both of you would agree to act like you were madly in love for thirty days, you will be amazed at how much in love you will be when the time is up.

Thoughts For the Lonely Nights

*Some survivors try to think their way through grief.
That doesn't work. Grief is a releasing process, a discovery process, a healing process...The brain must follow the heart at a respectful distance.*
      –Carol Staudacher
      A Time to Grieve

When You Feel Guilty

The one unhealthy place for anger to focus is inward. Far too often the feelings and frustrations have no place else to go, so they internalize and we start blaming ourselves. You can tell if this is happening to you because internalized anger turns into guilt. You will start obsessively playing the "If Only" game. Everyone plays a little of this game. We all think of what could have been done to make it better, but if your anger is internalizing you will be obsessive in the task. You will build elaborate schemes to prove it was your fault. This can start at a very early age. After the bombing in Oklahoma City, a little girl who was in the childcare center and survived decided she set off the bomb when she stepped on an electrical cord in the room.

I know of a person who decided he caused his brother's death. When he was a small boy he donated bone marrow so his brother could survive leukemia. It worked for a little while and then his brother died a very painful death. No one helped him deal with his feelings so they internalized and he grew to manhood in guilt. He is still a loner who finds it difficult to build close relationships.

Anger left alone will try to internalize. I talked with a man for several months who was caught up in a business merger and lost his job. After thirty years, he was fired with no warning and given no time to adjust. For weeks all I could get him to say was, "I should have been better prepared. I should have been ready." When I asked him what he said the day he was fired he told me he had not said anything. I asked him how he reacted to his company and found out he stayed around for two weeks to help them make the transition. He could not get angry at the company, so he ended up angry at himself. All of the anger internalized.

You may have built up some scenario very similar to this. How often do you start a conversation with "I should have?" How often do you say, "Why didn't I?" or, "If only I." These can be signs of internalized anger.

You cannot change the focus of anger by trying to change the focus of anger. That sounds backwards but it is true. The harder you argue with yourself, or the harder someone argues with you, the more intense the feelings become. It does very little good for someone to tell you it wasn't your fault. It will not help for someone to tell you that you can't let yourself think that way. These statements probably make you feel even more anger.

You change the focus of anger by recognizing that anger is what you are dealing with. If you can begin to look at and deal with the anger instead of trying to cure the focus it has taken, things will begin to change. It is like trying to cure a disease by working on the symptoms. The problem is you are angry and you have every right to be angry. If you can see that and say it, you can find some relief. It may not be instantaneous. It may not be dramatic. There are very few instant and dramatic cures in grief. Grief must be walked through and grown through. No drama here, but at least some quiet relief.

I hope you start this journal entry with, "I am angry! I have a right to be angry!! Matter of fact I am as MAD AS_____."

Truly, it is allowed to weep. By weeping, we disperse our wrath; and tears go through the heart, even like a stream.

−Ovid

When You Feel Dead Inside

There is a form of depression that does not exemplify itself by feeling blue or sad. It exemplifies itself by no feelings at all. If you experience this, you will feel detached and emotionally flat. You may want to care, but the normal feelings of care are not there. You are still interested but detached from any real feelings.

You will feel as if you are standing outside your own body watching you but having no emotional involvement in what is going on. You will continue to function but you won't really care one way or the other.

Your voice will flatten to near monotone and, try as you might, there will be no real emotional response found. It is like singing on a mountain in a high wind. There is no internal feedback and you feel all alone.

This is depression and it is very prevalent in grieving. Unfortunately it can leave us wondering if we have lost our ability to love or care.

If you are a woman with a family you might find this to be particularly troublesome. You are not accustomed to doing your work by rote. You take care of your family as an act of love and there is a great deal of emotion involved in the process. Now you give the care like a robot. This lack of feeling can make you feel a great deal of guilt. You may feel as if the family is noticing your lack of concern or care, but they probably are not doing so.

Many women have told me how maddening this can be. You want to love but there are no emotions to love with. You want to take care of your family, but you want to do so with the same feelings as before. One woman put it best. She said, "I want to *want to* again." Another woman said, "I feel gutted, I have nothing to give."

This lack of feelings seems to hit women the hardest. So much of the love and care women give is driven by emotions and feelings that they find it very hard to function without the "Want to."

Men also go through this period of deadness. Men hide it better and don't talk about it. They "suck it up" and go on but the dead feelings inside are there and they add to the pain.

What would you give to just feel again?

This is not the time for panic. Nor is it the time for deciding you will never love again, or never have feelings for your loved ones again. The feelings will return. This form of depression is caused by swallowed angers and frustrations. These do not go away, they build up inside and ultimately choke off feelings. As you talk through your angers and share your frustrations, your feelings will gradually return. Again, you need to keep your cussin' current.

These feelings will return much faster if you can keep from fighting yourself. The harder you try to feel, the more you kick yourself for not feeling, the more you feel you no longer love, the deeper the depression grows. You spend all of your energy fighting yourself and your lack of feelings. If you can relax a little and tell yourself that this is a normal response to the depression of grief and it will pass, the passing will come much sooner.

Until it passes, it is just a process of putting one foot in front of the other, and that is all right. There is no need to feel guilty because you don't feel right now. You might like to run and all you can do is crawl, but if that is what you can do right now then crawl. Give what you can and know the day will come when you will have much more to give.

Thoughts For the Lonely Nights

Life must go on
And the dead be forgotten
Life must go on
Though good men die;
Anne, eat your breakfast
Dan, take your medicine
Life must go on
I forget just why
        –Edna St. Vincent Millay

Thoughts For the Lonely Nights

Section II

The Questions

*Where there is sorrow
there is holy ground.*
　　　　–Oscar Wilde, *De Profundis*

Am I Doing it Right?

There will be no shortage of people who are willing to tell you how you are supposed to do your grieving. The ones who know the least will inevitably have the most advice to offer. There is even a pattern to how they will give this advice. First they will explain. They will have elaborate explanations as to why this happened, and how you should see it in a more positive light. Most of these explanations will be full of platitudes about how God took your loved one because He needed the best, or how much better off the person is now.

If the explanations don't work then you will begin to hear the arguments. "Now you can't let yourself think like that," or, "You must put this behind you and get on with your life." You will not only get tired of these; they will also make you angry.

If explanations and arguments do not suddenly make your grief go away, then will come the criticisms: *You are not trying to get well. You are just wallowing in your grief. You are hanging on to your grief in order to get attention.*

All of this comes from people who genuinely want to help. They are not being mean. They just don't know that grief is not something we should try to take away from people, that grief is something that must be walked through. And that every person must be free to react in their own way and for their own length of time.

There are no "right" ways to respond to grief. There is a right way for you and you should be free to find it. Everyone reacts to grief in a way that fits his or her particular needs. If what you are doing works, then it is right.

I have some friends who lost two sons in car accidents about ten years apart. Both were in college when they died. Both were remarkable young men. Both died during the Christmas holidays. The second death was more than their marriage and relationship could stand. I have watched these two people respond to these deaths for several years and they seem to be an example of the different approaches we take to grief.

I will call the husband J. C. He seemed to try to avoid the pain. He detached from life. He has not held a job since the last son died. He went through a long period of sleeping. He could not get enough sleep. His wife worried about his need for so much sleep and talked to me about how this was denial and avoidance. I agreed, but if that is what worked for him who could say it was wrong?

His avoidance took on many forms. He went through a period of being hyper-religious. He could not seem to get enough. He searched for evangelistic meetings especially those with great emotional outbursts. This did not last long, but for a little while it met his need and furnished him a "safe" place to be emotional.

Unfortunately his avoidance led him to medications and alcohol. I say "unfortunate" not as some sermon against drinking, but because pills and drink are especially dangerous while we are in grief. We tend to drink or take medication ahead of the pain—in case we hurt. Because we do not know if the pain is still there, we are afraid to stop and can become, at least, emotionally addicted.

The wife, I will call Mary, was just the opposite. She tried to stay busy enough to never have to be still or think. She began to travel,.to get involved in every kind of organization possible. She had no time for family and certainly no time for her husband. While he went to counseling, she would not take the time. While he read every book he could find, she read nothing. Her answer was to stay so busy she did not have time to hurt. That is also a form of avoidance, but that is the only way she knew to get through the pain.

You will find your own way. Some of the choices may be better than others, but you must find a way that works for you. I can tell you in a thousand different ways how you need to express your feelings, find help, go to a group or some other course of action, but the choice must be yours.

As I said in another part of this book, grief is transition. Where you are today is not where you will be tomorrow. These reactions will not be long lasting. These reactions do not define who you are. These reactions do not define your faith. All these reactions mean is that when you were turned upside down, your emotional being reacted in an effort to meet your needs at that time. That is all it means.

Thoughts For the Lonely Nights

...Grief changes the rules, and sometimes rearranges the combinations.
–Martha Whitmore Hickman
Healing After Loss

How Am I Supposed to Act?

I started studying grief when it dawned on me that as a minister I was doing a very bad job helping people who were in grief. The only way I knew to study the subject was to start meeting with a group of people who had recently lost a loved one. This may have been one of the first grief support groups ever formed, since at that time there was very little written or taught about grieving. One of the themes that kept coming up in that group was very surprising to me. The group kept asking how they were supposed to behave. The question took many forms, but the underlying quest was, "How do I behave now that I am in this strange position?"

One woman said, "I desperately need a new car, but I don't dare buy one because I can just hear them saying, 'Her husband isn't even cold and there she is out spending his money.'"

There seems to be an element of paranoia in grief. I am sure you have felt like all eyes are now directed at you. You feel like a marked person. Something strange has happened to you and now everyone is watching. These feelings are bound to make you cautious about what you do and how you are seen.

You would be amazed at how many people are not talking about you. There will always be the busy bodies who talk about everybody, but who listens? Your real friends will understand, and everyone else will not matter. You have more than enough to worry about right now without adding a load of pressure from people's opinions. Basically you should do what seems right for you right now and give no thought at all to public opinion.

You should make your own choice about when it is proper to go out socially. If you have lost a mate, there may come a time when you wish to build a relationship with someone else. There seems to be some unwritten rule that demands a wait of at least one year. I have never been able to figure out who made up this rule. Somehow the idea arose that anything less than one year did not show proper respect for the departed mate. The rule is wrong.

Sometimes early dating means the marriage was a pleasant experience and you would love to have that experience again. I will feel honored if my wife thought enough of being in love that she missed it and wanted to find it again.

You should date when and only when you feel like doing so. You should buy a car when and only when you feel like doing so. You should do what your inner feelings dictate. You are the only one who knows what you need and what works for you. There are no "experts" out there who have some knowledge about your grief that you do not have. Your instincts will guide you far better than anyone or anything else.

This book often says, "Feel what you feel." It also says, "Act like you feel like acting."

Thoughts For the Lonely Nights

I wonder–
   Does God gossip?
   Does He talk to other folks about me?
   If not, why do they think
      They know His way for me?
   If he does,
      I wish he would quit it.
                    –Doug Manning
                 Don't Take My Grief
                    Away From Me

What Do I Say?

Most of the help you will receive will come from your friends. Unfortunately most of the hurt you will receive will also come from your friends. They will say the wrong things. Some will not be there when you need them. In most cases, people in grief not only lose their loved one, they also lose friends. Some of your friends will not be able to stand the intimacy of the situation. Some will feel so inadequate about what to say to you or how to act toward you that they will not be able to force themselves to be with you.

It may help you to remember that a few months ago you did not know how to be a friend to a friend in grief either. You were just as lost as your friends are now. You may have said the same kinds of things that now make you angry to hear. Unfortunately, we have not done a very good job of studying grief and the needs of folks who are walking through it. This means our friends, who are the best source of help possible, are untrained and inadequate for the task.

I wish it were not so, but you may have to coach your friends and help them become comfortable with your grief. Tell them that it is all right to talk about your loved one. Teach them that you do not need or even want answers; all you need is ears. Let them know that if they "Hang around, Hug you, and Hush" they have been a source of great strength to you. If they can become relaxed and get over the fear of saying or doing the wrong things, they will be much more likely to be there when you need them. They will be much less likely to say the wrong things. Most wrong things are said because the friend thinks they have to say something, so they just talk, and out it comes.

At the same time, you will be finding new friends. People in grief seem to have a built-in radar system for finding each other. You will find new friends among those who have been through their own grief experience. You will be drawn to those who have been in the same kind of grief. If your child has died, you will find the most help from someone who has lost a child. No one feels as good to you as the person who has been there.

It is not only what others say to you, you will also find it hard to know what to say to them. What do you say when someone says, "How are you doing?" That presents a problem. Do they really want to know? How far should I go? I get so tired of saying, "I am doing all right" when I am dying inside. We learn to say these things to protect the ones who ask and ourselves. There are no hard and fast rules for what to say. I think it depends on who is asking. If it is someone you really don't want to talk to right then or it is not the place for such a conversation, then I think you pass it off with a "just fine." If it is someone you want to talk with, then I think you tell the truth. You must be prepared for some of the folks you try this on not knowing what to say next. If they don't know then at least they won't ask you the next time you meet. I think it is very proper to say, "I am having a very difficult time right now and I thank you for asking." If they know what to say next they will respond. If not, they will pass it off with a platitude and go on. I don't think you need to spend a great deal of time protecting the world.

I think it also depends on how you feel at that particular time. There are days when you can shake it off and there are days when you can't. It is all right to have a bad day. It is all right to not handle it well. It is all right to do it wrong. The person will get over it and they may just learn something in the process.

But the toughest thing is what do you say when someone says something that really hurts or makes you angry. That also depends on the person and the place, but there are times when you should respond in no uncertain terms. A friend of mine, whose husband died shortly before the holidays, attended a Christmas party she felt she had to attend. Her minister met her at the door and said, "Suzy, the secret is to just be happy." She took that one without comment. The minister's wife said, "I know this is a tough time for you but aren't you comforted by the thought that John is spending this Christmas in Heaven?" My friend said, "Hell no—he should be spending it here with me." I think that was most appropriate, even for the minister's wife. Don't you?

Thoughts For the Lonely Nights

*...To those who say they are sorry,
I gratefully say thank you, so am I. For those
who studiously avoid me, avoid looking me
straight on, avoid saying a single word,
I have nothing but contempt.
I know that I am being small and
meanspirited. I know that for many people
it is difficult to approach a person locked
in grief, but I know, too, that at this point
in what is left of my life I am not the most
forgiving person I know.*

–Ruth Coughlin
Grieving: A Love Story

When do I Clean the Closets?

I can almost guarantee that someone will tell you to clean out the clothes and possessions of your loved one as soon as possible. I don't know who came up with the idea that an empty closet does not give pain but a full one does. I think it came from the day when the conventional wisdom said that we should remove anything that reminds us of the loved one. The idea then was to take people's grief away from them. We now know that grief is a healing process that is to be embraced instead of avoided.

You should clean out the things when you feel like doing so. That may be quite soon, or it can take several years. I know a woman whose son died of suicide. She cleaned out his room within the first two months and turned the room into an office. That is typical of how she does everything. She makes quick decisions and moves on them immediately. Another friend of mine had a son that died of suicide about the same time. She did not move a thing in her son's room for five years. Both of these were correct in their approach to this issue. They did it in a way that fit them.

If grief is like peeling an onion, then deciding what to do with the possessions is part of that process. You give the things away a little at a time. There will be some things you can release quite early, but there probably will be those things you just must keep. These items have work to do. They remind you of the person and the wonderful experiences you shared. This becomes the foundation of memories that will become more precious every day you live. In time, even these things can be given to someone to use or they can be put away in some private place of memories.

A young man in our town died in an accident. The day before the funeral the father and father-in-law were in the front yard talking about how soon they could have an auction to "get rid" of the stuff. I asked them to wait until the wife decided to take such action. The father of the young man said, "But he has so many things that will be a memory for his wife and most of it she will never use." He pointed to the boat the young man had been so proud of and said, "Like that boat. That will be a constant reminder to her, and she will never use it. We need to sell the boat."

I said, "It is true that she will never use the boat, but she needs it maybe more than she needs any other of her husband's possessions. The day will come when she will take the boat out of her garage and put it somewhere in storage. That will be a big day for her. Some day she will decide to sell the boat and that will be an ever bigger day. That day she will know she is turning the corner and deciding to live again."

She lived down my street so I noticed the boat every time I drove past her house. About a year passed and one day she pulled the boat out of the garage and put it in storage. Another year passed and one day the boy's father said, "Do you remember when I wanted to have an auction and sell that boat?" I said that I did remember. He said, "I wish we had done so. She is going to sell it and I am going to buy it!" I guess, as time passed, he needed some things to hang onto while he peeled his own onion.

It might be helpful if you would write down the things you can't let go of and record what these things mean to you.

We do not remember days,
we remember moments.
            –Cesare Pavese

Thoughts For the Lonely Nights

How do I Handle the Holidays?

Grief is not a straight line. It has times of intense peaks and times when it seems to plateau at a constant state of hurt but not an intense wave. Most of the waves come with no warning and for no reason. There are some times when there is a reason for a wave to hit and one can be predicted. We can expect a peak at anniversaries and holidays.

Any anniversary will produce a peak in your grieving. About a month before any anniversary of birth, death, or marriage, a wave will begin to build. Usually you will not know what is happening, but you will become nervous and jittery. Your anger will seem to be right on the surface ready to explode at the slightest provocation. After a couple of weeks it will usually dawn on you that you are having these feelings because of the anniversary on the horizon. The rest of the time until the date you may spend in dreading the event. Most people report to me that the day is usually not as hard as they expected. The anticipation seems to be the tougher part.

The holidays can be very difficult. Most of our holidays are built on family and most families have traditional ways of celebrating each one. Most families start telling about any of the holidays with the sentence, "My family always…" After a loved one dies, these traditions have to change. You cannot face going through the same routines as if everything is the same. If your family always hung stockings, what are you going to do this Christmas? Hang all but one stocking? Hang them all and act like the death did not happen? The same can be said of the holidays of all religions.

This can create a struggle in the family. Most of the family will want everything back to normal. They want it over. You probably feel that they are minimizing your loss and the life of your loved one. You don't want it to be over. Nor can you even think of a time when anything will ever be normal again.

It may take great courage on your part, but you must decide what you can handle the first holiday seasons and structure your activities to meet your needs.

When one woman faced her first Christmas after the suicide of her son, she took the family to Disney World. The rest of the family could not understand or accept this. They put tremendous pressure on her, telling her that they needed her at home that Christmas more than ever. She held firm and they adjusted. She knew what she could handle and set it up for her comfort.

The same thing is true of all the other holidays. If you have always cooked the turkey at Thanksgiving, you may not want to do so this year. I think it is a good idea to write down what you feel like doing for these holidays, make a list for the family and then do exactly what you need to do. There will be other holiday seasons. And there will be new traditions built that in time will be just as meaningful as the ones that, of necessity, died along with your loved one.

*There is no greater
sorrow than to recall a time
of happiness in misery.*
        –Dante Alighieri

Why?

"Why did this happen?" is the number one question in grief. I could fill several pages with platitudes, clichés and beautiful phrases that would sound good and say nothing. We don't know why. No one knows why bad things happen to good people. I know that if bad things only happened to bad people we would all be good for the wrong reasons. I also know we would be in a desperate search to define the exact line that separates the good from the bad. "Just how good do I have to be?" would become the national obsession.

I do not know why this happened to you. I don't know why things happen to me. It takes all of the faith I can muster to think that one day I will know the answer and to be willing to wait until then. You can bet that the first day they have question and answer time in Heaven, I will be on the front row with my hand up.

In the meantime, we must live without any definitive answers. I know you must crave an answer to the why. Sometimes it becomes almost an obsession to us. Sometimes we feel if we could just get an answer to that question, it would make everything all right. I do not have an answer to your question. There is no way to make sense out of the nonsense life throws at us.

I do not know what caused your loss. I do know some things that were not the cause.

This did not happen to punish you. At one time, I had such a rigid concept of God that I was afraid to love my children too much for fear He would take them away from me as some kind of punishment for my faults. I searched the Bible on the subject of punishment. The Bible is a growing revelation. As you progress though it you see the folks discovering new ideas to replace old concepts. Early in the Bible there was the concept of "Our fathers have sinned and the children's teeth are set on edge." That bothered me for it seemed to say the children suffer for the acts of the parents. As I moved through the Bible the concept continued to change, until I came to Ezekiel 18. There the Bible says we should not say that anymore. It goes on to say, in my vernacular, that everyone is responsible for their own actions. God does not parlay one life against another. He does not sacrifice one life to get even with another life. Both are of equal importance. Both are loved.

Suddenly I saw the arrogance of my thoughts. I am so important that others would be hurt to save me? This did not happen to you to punish you. This did not happen to you to teach you a lesson. I don't know the answer, but I know that is not it.

I hope you will excuse this foray into the world of religion and I do recognize that you may not be into the same Bible or faith as I am. If you would allow me to do so I would like to sound preachy just long enough to tell you of my struggle toward some kind of answer to the "God question" in grief.

The only thing that I can come up with that makes sense, and it is far from perfect, is to see life as a large card game with fate dealing the cards. I had a struggle here. I wanted God to deal the cards and there be some way for me to get Him to deal me only good cards. I finally had to see it as life itself doing the dealing. God will not determine the cards. His role is to stand beside my chair and help me with whatever cards I get.

That is not a good answer. It is full of holes and problems. It is only my answer. It fits me and may not fit you at all. But all the other answers I tried left me with a *why* bigger than I could handle. Maybe, in time, you can write out an answer that makes sense to you. I hope so.

Thoughts For the Lonely Nights

He did not say: You will not be troubled, you will not be belabored, you will not be afflicted; but he said: You will not be overcome.
–Mother Julian of Norwich

Thoughts For the Lonely Nights

Section III

Needs

*...W*hen my wife got sick, I became more or less
isolated because she needed 24 hour-a-day
care. My son was out of town most of that year,
so I hardly ever saw him. I tried to talk to him once,
but it didn't work very well. Later I found a cartoon and
I told him "This is what your help was like."
The cartoon was a picture of a man on a psychiatrist's couch
and the psychiatrist is flailing his arms and saying
"Pack up your troubles in your old kit bag and Smile! Smile!
Smile!" He didn't know what I was going through and I
didn't know what was happening with him—grieving
for his mother. We were just a pair of human beings
trying to find our way.

–Scott Campbell with Phyllis R. Silverman
Widower

The Power of an Ear

The first and most important thing you need in finding your way through your grief is a safe set of ears. The second most important thing is another safe set of ears. Matter of fact, you need about five sets of good ears.

Finding these ears will not be easy. People who are willing to just listen, without trying to tell you how to feel or think, are very rare. People who can be comfortable in the intimacy of shared feelings are wonderful treasures. Safe ears are those that are willing to listen without trying to change the way you feel by changing the way you think. They do not try to "put the best spin" on your pain. They do not feel some great urge to be a wonderful advisor who has the answers. They understand your need is someone who will listen.

Getting comfortable doing the talking may be just as difficult as finding a set of ears to talk with. It must sound far too simplistic when counselors say, "You need to talk it out." Surely there is more to it than that. There must be some other help in this pain—maybe some formula or some medication or even an exercise or mantra. Just saying all you need to do is *talk* sounds like there really is no cure, so just keep talking until we find something better to suggest.

There are things that happen to you when you talk or express feelings that do not happen any other way. When you are heard, I mean really heard, by a safe set of ears you:

...Bleed Off Anger

You may have already experienced this effect. Have you been very angry, but when you told a friend about your anger you somehow couldn't make it sound as bad as it was? Finally you muttered something like,

"Well, you had to be there." But you can't feel as angry about it after that event. That is the power of the ear. You were bleeding off the anger as you talked. We reduce anger as we express it. Talking is best, but writing is also helpful. This might be a good time for you to stop and write out your angers: The things that hurt, the things that frustrate, the things that seem to cut into your heart.

...Learn

Sometime in your life you have been told that you are not learning when your mouth is open. Somehow we developed the idea that learning happens when someone else is telling us things. Just the opposite is true. You are doing your best learning when you are talking. The learning process works best when we have a thought, wallow it around in our minds for a while, then when we begin to talk it out it becomes ours. Thoughts internalize when we share them. Too much of our knowledge is in our heads and never gets into our emotions. Knowledge is just information passing through until we grab it, talk or write how we feel about it, and claim it for our own.

All of the information you hear or read about grief will be just so much passing knowledge until you find some safe ears to share it with. I urge people to make lists of things they need to talk out with a friend. Too often we get caught up in small talk and forget what we wanted to say. It does not matter whether the friend agrees with what you are thinking or saying. The goal is to give you a chance to think it through while you are talking it out. That is real learning.

...Receive Insight

I continue to be amazed at how counseling works. Most of the time the counselor has no idea whether or not any good is being accomplished. When someone tells me how much help they have received, I am always tempted to ask them what they are talking about and how it happened. Counseling is not a process of my telling a person some great truths. Counseling is a process of my giving them the setting to talk and, as they talk, insights seem to surface. Last week a woman called to tell me I had helped her daughter tremendously. Her daughter could now understand what she was feeling and see a way to handle the issues that seemed so insurmountable before we talked. All I remember was a nice pleasant talk with nothing remarkable happening, but in the process of talking she had found insight.

The same will happen to you. As you talk it out, ideas will just come to you. As you talk it out, feelings will change. Problems that seem to have no answers can become understandable. Anger toward others can somehow lessen as you suddenly see the other side of the issue. This information is available from inside of you and nowhere else. It is there already. You do not have to learn it; you just need to discover it. The discoveries happen through the use of safe ears. Writing out what you feel and then sharing what you have written with safe ears can be the easiest way to create these times of discovery.

...She used to rock me in her arms, consoling my pain, but not only consoling, for she seemed to take my sorrow to her own breast, and I realized that if I had not been able to bear the society of other people, it was because they all played the comedy of trying to cheer me with forgetfulness. Instead she said:
"Tell me about Deidre and Patrick," and made me repeat to her all their little sayings and ways, and show her their photos which she kissed and cried over. She never said, "Cease to grieve," but she grieved with me, and, for the first time since their death, I felt I was not alone."

–Isadora Duncan
speaking about her friend,
Eleanora Duse, after the deaths
of her two children
My Life

Thoughts For the Lonely Nights

Ears Give Significance

When bad things happen to us the first thing we want, and need, to do is to establish the significance of that event. We become like a little child with a cut finger going around showing everyone the "boo-boo." When everyone has seen the sore place the incident will be forgotten. But, when the child is trying to show it off he or she will be persistent to the point of being obnoxious. That is human nature. When things happen to us we just must tell someone or, better still, everyone.

A fellow passenger on an airport shuttle bus going out to an airplane suddenly said, "I hope this plane is on time: I am on my way to my mother's funeral. I have had a terrible time trying to get tickets and get myself ready. She died very suddenly although she had a stroke several months ago." She continued on until the bus arrived at the plane. I am sure she told her story all the way to her destination. What would make a grown woman tell such private things to total strangers? She needed to establish the significance of what she was experiencing.

You face the same need. You need to tell anyone and everyone what has happened to you. That sounds selfish or at least self-centered, but it is neither. It is simply the first step toward having the ability to cope with your loss. You need to talk about what has happened to you, and you need someone to hear it, without trying to "put the best face on it."

The opposite of significance is trivialization. You do not want to be trivialized. Having someone make light of what you are experiencing is terribly frustrating. When someone says, "It could be worse," or, "Your loved one is in a better place and would not want you to be sad," or maybe even worse, "God will not put any more on you than you can bear," it makes you angry. It angers because these statements trivialize instead of giving significance to your pain.

Establishing significance after the loss of a loved one takes place at three levels.

First you need to establish the significance of your loss:
What has happened to you
What this loss means to your future
How this loss will affect your family
How this loss will affect your financial well-being

All of that sounds like a gigantic pity party. It sounds as if thinking or saying these things will make you feel worse. Somehow we developed the idea that sympathy makes grief worse, or to sympathize is like pouring gasoline on a fire. The result of this fallacy is to not talk about the very things we need to talk about. All of these issues become the "elephant" in the room that everyone acts like they don't see.

Talking out the significance of your loss is the healthiest thing you can possibly do. My hope is that you will find a safe person who will not try to *spin doctor* what you say, but will just allow you to vent these feelings for as long as you need.

Then you need to establish the significance of the person you have lost. It seems as if you need to inventory the loss before you can grieve it. You do not know what you have lost until the person is gone. It is then that the real significance of the person can be discovered. We take so much for granted. We accept the personality of the person without thinking how much they mean. When they are alive we accept them as a total package and do not notice each little part they play in our lives. After they are gone, we begin to notice how much we miss each of those little parts.

You think of new things they did or meant almost every hour. You will think of things you want to tell them. Things they said that you barely noticed at the time but now ring in your mind like a bell: *the way they smiled, the way they walked, their unique smell, the warmth of their presence, their meaning in your life.* These are the things you need to remember and talk about. That is called establishing their significance.

That is the second step toward coping with your loss.

Then there is the social significance. You need to know how much your loved one meant to others. It feels wonderful when friends tell you how much your loved one meant to them. When they tell stories and recreate meaningful times they shared, you cry while feeling a sense of release inside. People who suffer the death of a child are especially blessed when someone calls the child's name and is comfortable talking about the child. Flowers sent, cards written, and phone calls long after everyone else has forgotten, all have meaning because they are saying your loved one had significance and that significance is still alive and still remembered.

If we were sitting together tonight, and you were in pain, I would ask you to tell me what the loss means to you, and about the person who has died. You would cry, of course. This would bring up memories that are painful to recount. I hope I would avoid the urge to make it all better: to explain it away, to try to cheer you up. That would make me feel better, but it would not make your pain go away; you would talk, I would listen. I would wonder if I was doing you any good at all. I would fear that I was making it worse. You would feel a strange sense of warmth inside the pain. Tomorrow you would feel washed out and detached. The next day you would feel a little better and somehow lifted up. For our talk would have been one of the many times you need for establishing the significance of this loss.

I cannot be there, but we can make part of it happen with your pen writing out the feelings this conversation has described.

...And ever has it been that love knows not its own depth until the hour of separation.
–Kahlil Gibran
The Prophet

Thoughts For the Lonely Nights

The Power of Being Heard

If we can establish significance, we can move on. If we can't do so we tend to keep trying to do so until the feelings gradually become an obsession. I have become intrigued with the causes of long-term hurts and grudges. A grudge does not happen because someone is too hardheaded to forgive. A grudge happens when someone is hurt and can never establish the significance of that hurt. They keep trying and get hurt even deeper because no one will listen or understand. Over time that hurt becomes a grudge that can dominate a life.

Significance happens when we are understood. I love the word "understanding." Not that anyone can really understand how you feel. Nor will you appreciate hearing folks say that they understand exactly how you feel. Most of the time that will make you angry. I love "understanding" in the sense that when people really listen and try to understand, something wonderful happens inside of us. The longer I live the more impressed I am with that word, for the bottom line is we just want to be understood. We want to have our feelings legitimized and our thoughts given credence.

The Biblical story of Job is a picture of a man seeking someone to simply allow him to feel what he felt—to give credence to his feelings and legitimize his thoughts. He had two friends who listened for seven days and never heard a thing he said. Then they opened their mouths and added to his pain. Instead of feeling what he felt they began long explanations for what had happened to him. Instead of accepting his thoughts, they began to argue with him. They thought they could change how he felt by changing the way he thought and Job was subjected to hours of long diatribes that added to his pain.

It sounds simplistic, but what you need more than any other thing is for someone to hear you out. Understanding does not mean they feel what you feel. Understanding means they accept your feelings as valid and all right for you to feel. Nothing that I know of can do so much nor feel so wonderful as simply being understood.

Most of the time all we want is presence. Someone to just be there. Someone who will allow us to say anything we feel like saying without thinking they must correct us or save us from ourselves. Someone who will simply hurt with us can do wonders. We tend to be afraid of sympathy but there is nothing more healing. Sympathy means it is all right to feel the way you feel. You deserve it. If you can find a place and a person who will allow you this freedom without trying to change the way you think or feel, you can find the way through your grief made much easier and more meaningful.

Now is the time for some coaching of friends. Ask them to read these two chapters on significance and understanding so they will know what role they can play. Then unload on them. Wallow in your grief until you have worked through the significance and feel understood.

It might be helpful to make a list of the friends you think can do such a service. It might also be helpful to continue making a list of the things you need to say.

There's an elephant in the room.
It is large and squatting, so it is hard to get around it.
Yet we squeeze by with "How are you?" and "I'm fine"...
And a thousand other forms of trivial chatter.
We talk about weather.
We talk about work.
We talk about everything else–except the elephant in the room.
There's an elephant in the room.
We all know it is there.
We are thinking about the elephant as we talk together.
It is constantly on our minds.
For, you see, it is a very big elephant.
It has hurt us all.
But we do not talk about the elephant in the room.
Oh, please, say "Barbara" again.
Oh, please, let's talk about the elephant in the room.
For if we talk about her death.
Perhaps we can talk about her life.
Can I say "Barbara" to you and not have you look away?
For if I cannot, then you are leaving me
Alone...In a room...
With an elephant.

Turning the Corner in the Way You Cope

If grief is like peeling an onion, then the last layer of the onion is reconstruction. There will come a time when you decide to live again. You will not be well. You will not be back to normal. There will never be a time when you don't remember or hurt. There will come a time when you turn the corner in the way you cope. You will learn to live with a new relationship to the one you loved, a relationship of memories and spirit.

Deciding to live again may well be a dramatic event. You will probably know when it takes place. There may be something you cannot handle now that you will realize is no longer a problem. It may be something you cannot dispose of or put away. A chair you cannot sit on. A room you cannot visit; pictures that are hidden. Then, for no apparent reason, it is no longer a problem.

One woman told me she could not sit in her husband's chair for almost two years after he died. She also could not move the chair or any of the things her husband kept on the table next to it. His glasses remained, though the sight of them was painful to her. His pipe lay on the ashtray, though the smell brought back so many memories. She wondered if she would ever be able to sit in the chair or move the things. One night it was suddenly all right. She sat there for a long time and felt close to her husband. She wanted to move the things away and redecorate the room. What was unthinkable the day before became perfectly all right and logical that day. She had turned the corner in a rather dramatic and sudden way.

Your decision may not be that dramatic at all. A friend told me as she was walking to her car after church one Sunday it suddenly hit her that she had to decide right then whether to live or die. She decided to live again, and that was her turning point in the way she coped with her loss.

You may get up to this point many times before you turn the corner. Or you may turn it suddenly without warning. In your own way, in your own time, and after your own lonely nights, you will walk through this lonesome valley and learn to live again. What a thought.

Thoughts For the Lonely Nights

In the beginning, memory is a nightstalker and imagination its cruel accomplice. Why, why? What if, what if? Lying tangled and sweating in a nightmare of lost possibilities, we await the mercy of morning.

The dawn brings an unlikely companion: the past has become a friend. This is the surprise we have been waiting for. Suddenly there is no struggle to hide from memory and imagination. Suddenly memory is sweet and imagination liberating.

—Molly Fumia
Safe Passage: Words to Help the Grieving Hold Fast

Memories

My grandmother died in 1960. At least they said she did. But no one is dead until they are forgotten, and we will never forget her. The night before her funeral my father suggested that we all go down and visit with Mamma Hoyle. We sat in the funeral home and told stories around her casket long into the night. We laughed and cried and learned things about her we never knew before. We buried her body the next day, but she is still alive among us through those stories. Every time the family gets together we tell Momma Hoyle stories. I not only know the stories that will be told, I know the order in which they will be told. And through those stories she lives. My children know her well, and some were born after she died. Their children will know her as well as many future generations. We never forget those who love us and share their lives in our lives.

We live on in two ways—in life beyond life and in the lives of those who love us. Your loved one will live in the memories you carry and those carried by the extended family and friends. Memories are strange and wonderful things. In those first hurting times of grief the memories are the things that cause the hurt. You think of wonderful times that will be no more and your whole body feels hollow and empty. You cannot bear to let these memories linger in your mind more than a moment. The pain is too great.

Gradually, as you walk through the process, you can begin to keep the memories in your mind for growing lengths of time. They still hurt. They still bring tears. Some of them cause pain for days, but you can tolerate them for a little while.

As time passes the memories become more of a comfort than a pain. You can begin to welcome them into your consciousness. You can begin to share them with friends and family. They don't hurt as much as they once did.

There will come a time when nothing will be more comforting than a session of story telling about your loved one. When a friend tells of some experience they remember, it will feel warm inside. When the family gathers there will always be a time for story telling. It will not be an organized event, it will just happen and be all the sweeter because it was so natural.

Isn't it strange that the very thing that now causes you the most pain will one day give you the most comfort? There was an old gospel song called *Precious Memories*. The title may sound corny but memories really are precious.

This book can be the beginning of collecting your treasure. A place for you to write out what your loved one meant and what you will remember the most, a place for some stories. A place to list some of the crisis you faced together, a place to write out how brokenhearted you are from the loss. There may even be a space for some stories told by special friends or family members.

If you have lost a child, these pages are waiting for you to lovingly describe the significance of your child. One woman said, "The grief following the death of a child is a process of trying not to say good-bye. You feel like the child did not live long enough to establish their significance and you must establish it for them."

I only wish we could sit together someday. I could tell you Momma Hoyle stories and you could tell me the wonderful stories of your loved one.

In the rising of the sun
*   and in its going down*
We remember them;
In the blowing of the wind and
*   in the chill of winter,*
We remember them;
In the opening of the buds and
*   in the warmth of summer,*
We remember them;
In the rustling of leaves
*   and the beauty of autumn,*
We remember them;
In the beginning of the year
*   and when it ends,*
We remember them;
So long as we live, they too
*   shall live,*
For they are now a part of us as
We remember them.
                    −Gates of Prayer
            Reform Judaism Prayerbook

About the Author
Doug Manning

Doug's career has included minister, counselor, business executive, author and publisher. He and his wife, Barbara, were parents to four daughters and long-term caregivers to three parents.

After thirty years in the ministry, Doug began a new career in 1982 and has devoted his time to writing, counseling and leading seminars in the areas of grief and elder care. His publishing company, InSight Books, Inc., specializes in books, video and audio productions specifically designed to help people face some of the toughest challenges of life.

Doug has a warm, conversational style in which he shares insights from his various experiences. Sitting down to read a book from Doug is like having a long conversation with a good friend.

Qutoes Bibliography

Campbell, Scott and Phyllis R. Silverman. *Widower.* Baywood Publishing Co.

Couglin, Ruth. *Grieving: A Love Story.* Random House, Inc. 1993.

Fumia, Molly. *Safe Passage: Words to Help the Grieving Hold Fast and Let Go.* Conari Press. 1992.

Lindbergh, Anne Morrow. *Hour of Gold, Hour of Lead.* Harcourt Brace and Company. 1973.

McNees, Pat, comp. *Dying, A Book of Comfort.* Garden City, New York: Doubleday Direct, Inc. 1996. ISBN 0-446-67400-1

Selected Resources from InSight

Building Memories: Planning a Meaningful Funeral
Grief's Second Mile: Beyond the First Year
Journey of Grief DVD (also available streaming - Spanish & French subtitles)
*Lean On Me Gently: Helping the Grieving Child**
The Power of Presence: Helping People Help People Book or DVD
Sacred Moments: A Minister Speaks About Funerals
Special Care Series (also availabel in Spanish)
*Thoughts for the Holidays**
Thoughts for the Grieving Christian book/journal or CD

* Also available as e-Books from your favorite vendor

For a more information contact:
InSight Books, Inc.
800.658.9262 or 405.810.9501
OrdersAndInfo@InSightBooks.com
www.InsightBooks.com
Sign up for our eNewsletter and follow us on Facebook